ON LOVE

Books by Edward Hirsch

Poetry

LAY BACK THE DARKNESS   2003

ON LOVE   1998

EARTHLY MEASURES   1994

THE NIGHT PARADE   1989

WILD GRATITUDE   1986

FOR THE SLEEPWALKERS   1981

Prose

THE DEMON AND THE ANGEL: SEARCHING FOR THE SOURCE
OF ARTISTIC INSPIRATION   2002

HOW TO READ A POEM AND FALL IN LOVE WITH POETRY   1999

RESPONSIVE READING   1999

Editor

TRANSFORMING VISION: WRITERS ON ART   1994

ON LOVE

POEMS BY

Edward Hirsch

ALFRED A. KNOPF   NEW YORK   2002

Copyright © 1998 by Edward Hirsch

All rights reserved under International and Pan-American Copyright Conventions. Published in the United States by Alfred A. Knopf, Inc., New York, and simultaneously in Canada by Random House of Canada Limited, Toronto. Distributed by Random House, Inc., New York.

www.randomhouse.com

Knopf, Borzoi Books, and the colophon are
registered trademarks of Random House, Inc.

Grateful acknowledgment is made to the editors of the following publications where these poems—some of which have been substantially revised—first appeared:

American Poetry Review: "Tristan Tzara," "Milena Jesenská"
Antaeus: "Days of 1968"
Chicago Review: "Orphic Rites"
DoubleTake: "The Poet at Seven," "Denis Diderot," "Zora Neale Hurston"
Five Points: "Federico García Lorca"
The Kenyon Review: "A Fundamentalist," "Husband and Wife"
The New Republic: "Hotel Window"
The New Yorker: "Blue Hydrangea"
The New York Times Op Ed Page: "American Summer"
The Paris Review: "Ocean of Grass," "Iowa Flora," "The Idea of the Holy," "The Burning of the Midnight Lamp," "Giacomo Leopardi," "Heinrich Heine," "Charles Baudelaire," "Margaret Fuller," "Ralph Waldo Emerson," "Colette"
Poetry: "Oscar Ginsburg," "Guillaume Apollinaire," "Marina Tsvetaeva"
Raritan: "Gertrude Stein"
Slate: "A Painting of Pan"
The Yale Review: "The Unnaming"

Library of Congress Cataloging-in-Publication Data

Hirsch, Edward.
On love : poems / by Edward Hirsch.
p. cm.
ISBN 0-375-70260-1
I. Title.
PS3558.I6405   1998   97-49460
811'.54—dc21   CIP

Manufactured in the United States of America
Published June 10, 1998
First Paperback Edition Published Januuary 2000
Reprinted Twice
Fourth Printing, October 2002

. . . my being is but thine own—

Fused from its separateness by ecstasy.

Thomas Hardy, "She, to Him, IV"

Contents

Blue Hydrangea   3
The Poet at Seven   4
Ocean of Grass   5
Iowa Flora   6
American Summer   7
Days of 1968   8
The Burning of the Midnight Lamp   9
Orphic Rites   12
The Unnaming   14
Hotel Window   15
Idea of the Holy   17
Two (Scholarly) Love Poems   19
A Painting of Pan   21
A Fundamentalist   22
Husband and Wife   24

2 ON LOVE

Prologue   28
Denis Diderot   29
Giacomo Leopardi   31
Heinrich Heine   32
Charles Baudelaire   34
Margaret Fuller   36
Ralph Waldo Emerson   38
George Meredith   40
Lafcadio Hearn   44

CONTENTS

Oscar Wilde   4

Tristan Tzara   4

Guillaume Apollinaire   5

Milena Jesenská   5

D. H. Lawrence   5

H. D.   5

Federico García Lorca   5

Robert Desnos   6

Gertrude Stein   6

Dr. X   6

Bertolt Brecht   7

Marina Tsvetaeva   7

Zora Neale Hurston   7

Oscar Ginsburg   8

Paul Valéry   8

Colette   8

1

Blue Hydrangea

Mop-headed transplant from late summer,
hydrangea macrophylla, blue wave,
you were colorless when I brought you home,
as if the ocean had travelled a great distance
and washed-out in your veins.

Secret white mirror of my convalescence,
echo of forgotten twilights
and long ago dawns, lost Rilkean cousin,
how many nights have I sat alone with you,
longing for transformation?

But nothing happens. Blue hydrangea,
most soiled of household gods,
I need a sudden flare of color, a torch
to explode through the sterile florets
and burn away the night.

The Poet at Seven

He could be any seven-year old on the lawn,
holding a baseball in his hand, ready to throw.
He has the middle-class innocence of an American,

except for his blunt features and dark skin
that mark him as a Palestinian or a Jew,
his forehead furrowed like a question,

his concentration camp eyes, nervous, grim,
and too intense. He has the typical
blood of the exile, the refugee, the victim.

Look at him looking at the catcher for a sign—
so violent and competitive, so unexceptional,
except for an ancestral lamentation,

a shadowy, grief-stricken need for freedom
laboring to express itself through him.

Ocean of Grass

The ground was holy, but the wind was harsh
and unbroken prairie stretched for hundreds of miles
so that all she could see was an ocean of grass.

Some days she got so lonely she went outside
and nestled among the sheep, for company.
The ground was holy, but the wind was harsh

and prairie fires swept across the plains,
lighting up the country like a vast tinderbox
until all she could see was an ocean of flames.

She went three years without viewing a tree.
When her husband finally took her on a timber run
she called the ground holy and the wind harsh

and got down on her knees and wept inconsolably,
and lived in a sod hut for thirty more years
until the world dissolved in an ocean of grass.

Think of her sometimes when you pace the earth,
our mother, where she was laid to rest.
The ground was holy, but the wind was harsh
for those who drowned in an ocean of grass.

Iowa Flora

(In Memory of Amy Clampitt)

We thought we were having an indigenous childhood
splashed with Indian paintbrush and grassy knolls
thickened by birdfoot violets and ordinary goldenrod,

but we kept finding noxious alien weeds in the hills—
quackgrass and thistle, European morning glory
that no state legislation could control.

We inherited pioneer grasses high as a prairie
schooner, but there were also fresh settlements
of bog flowers and refugees from the sea-

coast marshes, silky-leaved Virginia plants
and Texas marigolds, imported seeds and ornamentals,
weeds from the wasted villages of other continents.

Nature consists of immigrants and mongrels:
you showed us how to prize coincidence and impurity
in wayward fields, the deserted and marginal . . .

I went down to the swamp to mourn for you, Amy,
and it was as if Providence led me to the place
where I stumbled upon yellow swamp betony

and pink foxglove mingled with something nameless
(*unfathomable the mystery before us,* you said)
and the shining, cup-flowered grass of Parnassus.

American Summer

Each day was a time clock that scarcely moved,
a slow fist punching us in, punching us out,
electric heat smoldering in the purple air,

but each night was a towering white fly ball
to center field—"a can of corn"—coming down
through stars glittering above the diamond.

Each day was a pair of heavy canvas gloves
hoisting garbage cans into an omnivorous mouth
that crept through thoroughfares and alleys,

but each night was the feeling of a bat
coming alive in your hands, it was lining
the first good pitch for a sharp single.

That summer I learned to steal second base
by getting the jump on right-handed pitchers
and then sliding head-first into the bag.

I learned to drive my father's stick shift
and to park with my girlfriend at the beach,
our headlights beaming and running low.

I was a sixteen-year-old in the suburbs
and each day was another lesson in working,
a class in becoming invisible to others,

but each night was a Walt Whitman of holidays,
the clarity of a whistle at five p.m.,
the freedom of walking out into the open air.

Days of 1968

She walked through Grant Park during the red days of summer.
One morning she woke up and smelled tear gas in her hair.

She liked Big Brother and the Holding Company, Bob Dylan,
Sly & the Family Stone, The Mothers of Invention.

When Jimi Hendrix played *Purple Haze* in a Jam Session
she had a vision of the Trail of Tears and the Cherokee Nation.

She dropped acid assiduously for more than a year.
She sang, "I want to take you higher and higher,"

and dreamt of cleansing the doors of perception.
After she joined the Sky Church I never saw her again . . .

Days of 1968, sometimes your shutters open
and I glimpse a star gleaming in the constellations.

I can almost reach up and snag her by the hand.
I can go to her if I don't look back at the ground.

The Burning of the Midnight Lamp

Listening to *Purple Haze* and *The Wind Cries Mary,*
Let Me Stand Next to Your Fire and *Manic Depression,*

I am drifting undersea toward strobe lights
and feedback, the dreamy, acoustic waves of 1969.

Remember how you explained those dirty sounds—
the two-note riff banned by the Spanish Inquisition,

the hammer-ons and pull-offs, the sharpened ninth?
Is it tomorrow or just the end of time?

I've forgotten nothing. Any moment I'll cross
the campus near the dormitory where you've moved in

with another man; I'll pause under the window trembling
with volume—a betrayer betrayed and turning back

to the raw, metallic, bristling taste of wind.
The morning is dead and the day is too

There's nothing left here to lead me, but the velvet moon
(you always liked the wah-wah pedal on that song).

. . .

Someone is playing *Voodoo Child* and *House Burning Down*,
checking the chord progression in *Spanish Castle Magic*

and the octaves in *Third Stone from the Sun.*
Another is blasting *Crosstown Traffic* from a lounge

where darkness branches into maroon rivers
and cigarette butts flare into the stars.

No more parties with our friends eating seeds
and lacing punch, smoking joints in a dim room

where you go on talking about sinister bent strings
and dive-bombing sounds, the devil invoked

in the interval of a tritone or flattened fifth.
No more waiting for you to return to me

(*that forgotten earring lying on the floor*)
through a downpour of left-handed notes.

But sometimes when I close my eyes
I see your body fading back into shadows.

. . .

As a child, Jimi Hendrix watched his soul floating
away from his torso, looking down at himself

from a different realm. He was awake but slipping
mindlessly through another dimension, the astral plane.

That's how you felt about LSD and STP,
those ten-milligram doses of the sublime.

We were looking for fire escapes: ladders
and watchtowers spiraling up from the ground.

But that year as I smoldered within my body
and you tripped through the acid nights

Orpheus stomped microphones and humped speakers,
smashing amplifiers on stage after stage

as though he could whammy the Underworld
into submission and subdue the Furies

while darkness vibrated around him
and electric guitars exploded in flames.

Orphic Rites

(Hart Crane, 1899–1933)

Plato says the gods sent him weeping away, empty-
Handed from Hades, deceiving him with a shadow
Of his bride, not returning her actual body

Because he was only a poor-spirited musician
Enchanting himself into the underworld
Rather than joining her the proper way, by dying.

Orpheus descended through the gate of Tainaron
And sang so poignantly of his lost wife
He set even the bottomless spaces grieving,

But he was not going to pollute the altars
With blood or donate his lyre to the Shades.
He was not ready to swallow oblivion

Or share the destiny of the dead spirits
Whose bodies were scattered to nether regions
And whose mouths were transformed into fog.

That is when he was exiled among the Thracians
Where he sang of a country sealed behind him
Like the origin of all things, which is death.

Some say he founded a School of Darkness
And wandered through secret caverns devising
Rituals of initiation, canons of purity,

All the while denouncing the hydra-headed monster
Time, sleeping above ground, and mourning
A face he could no longer find in the light

And a voice he could no longer hear calling
Through a fissure in the earth. Therefore,
He turned to men's bodies for consolation,

Prohibited the eating of animals, and praised
Drunken ecstasy that leads back to the divine . . .
Some say the Maenads destroyed him, taking revenge,

But I believe he flung himself into the water
So that his head could go sailing home, singing
Under a cloudy sky brimming with erasures.

The Unnaming

(Amherst, 1860)

She walked through the house, taking away its names.
The high ceilings will no longer be called ceilings,
She thought, and the parlors will no longer be parlors.

There will be no more bedchambers or sitting rooms,
No more Sheraton bureaus, Franklin stoves, cherry-wood tables.
There would be no more time for commonplace aspirations

As she moved through the halls in a rapture of unmaking,
Withdrawing the designations, taking down doors and windows,
The heavy stairs she had climbed so many times before,

Holding the banister and dreaming of a carpenter
Who had carved the boards from a sacrificial tree
So she could go back and forth to a white study.

She took courage from Eve's deleting of the names
Adam had given the beasts, haunting Eden
By returning the animals to their first splendor

And treating the garden as a page for revisions.
She took heart from a snowfall blanketing the earth,
An oblivion outside matching the oblivion within.

She, too, moved through a garden of cancellations
(*No more monarchies of Queen Anne's lace,* she chanted
To herself, *no more dead elms branching into heaven*)

And what was when she felt the dizzying freedom
Of a world cut loose from the affixed Word or words,
Appallingly blank, waiting to be renamed.

Hotel Window

Aura of absence, vertigo of non-being—
could I ever express what happened?
It was nothing, really, or next to nothing.

I was standing at the window at dusk
watching the cabs or the ghosts of cabs
lining up on the other side of the street

like yellow ferryboats waiting to cross
a great divide. All afternoon the doorman
whistled through the shadows, Charon

slamming doors and shouting orders
at traffic piling up along the curb.
People got into cars and disappeared—

ordinary people, tourists, businessmen—
while fog thickened the city's features
and emptied out the color. I don't know

how long I stood there as darkness
inhabited air itself, but suddenly,
when it happened, everything seemed dis-

jointed, charged with non-existence,
as if a vast, drowned lake was rising
invisibly—permanently—from the ground.

At the same time nothing really changed,
footsteps still echoed in the hallway
and laughter flared up the stairwell,

the passengers flinging themselves into cabs
never noticed they were setting forth
on a voyage away from their bodies.

I felt within a sickening emptiness—
intangible, unruly—and I remember
lying down on the floor of the room . . .

Then the phone rang and it was over.
Nothing happened—it took only a moment—
and it was dizzying, relentless, eternal.

Idea of the Holy

(New York City, 1975)

Out of the doleful city of Dis
rising between the rivers

Out of the God-shaped hole in my chest
and the sacred groves of your body

Out of stars drilled through empty spaces
and Stones in My Passway at four a.m.

All those hours studying under the lamp
the First Cause and the Unmoved Mover

the circle whose circumference is
everywhere and whose center is nowhere

the Lord strolled under the oak tree at Mamre
at the hottest moment of the day

the Lord vacated a region within himself
and recoiled from the broken vessels

a God uncreated or else a God withdrawn
a God comprehended is no God

Out of subway stations and towering bridges
Out of murky waters and the wound of chaos

Out of useless walks under fire escapes
Be friends to your burning

I saw the sun convulsed in clouds
and the moon candescent in a ring of flame

souls I saw weeping on streetcorners
in a strangeness I could not name

O falling numinous world at dusk
O stunned and afflicted emptiness

After three days and nights without sleep
I felt something shatter within me

then I lay down on my cot motionless
and sailed to the far side of nothing

Two (Scholarly) Love Poems

1 *Dead Sea Scrolls*

I was like the words
        on a papyrus apocryphon
                buried in a cave at Qumran,

and you were the scholar
        I had been waiting for
                all my life, the one reader

who unravelled the scrolls
        and understood the language
                and deciphered its mysteries.

TWO (SCHOLARLY) LOVE POEMS

2   *A Treatise on Ecstasy*

Touching your body
        I was like a rabbi pouring
                over a treatise on ecstasy,
                        the message hidden in the scrolls.

I remember our delirium
        as my fingers moved backwards
                across the page, letter by letter,
                        word by word, sentence by sentence.

I was a devoted scholar
        patiently tracing the secret
                passages of a mysterious text.
                        Our room became a holy place

as my hands trembled
        and my voice shook
                when I recited the blessings
                        of a book that burst into flames.

A Painting of Pan

("He who feeds")

I wasn't afraid of the painting of Pan
mounting the nymph from behind, seizing her.
I wasn't afraid of crossing the room
to study it, under the burning chandelier.

And when I saw the god's animal eyes—
glittering, heedless, intent—
and how the girl looked back at him
with a half-curious, half panicky stare

I remembered how you looked at me
across the reeling party that night
and how, later, when I touched your arm
something flickered on your face—

open and feral, frank. A hunted look.
A kind of tenderness toward the hunter.
A perception of everything sordid
that was going to happen between us.

Look at me, I said later in bed,
and you looked up with my wet food
smeared across your parted lips
and I saw it flickering again—

that creature trapped in your eyes,
that tenderness toward the predator
I'd become, one who feeds off others,
that look of haunted recognition.

A Fundamentalist

It was just a dump really,
    a salt-sprayed room
        in a transient hotel
            falling into the open sea,

but we loved its tackiness—
    its crippled flamingos
        and blustering neon sign:
            Wellcome to U Travellers!

It was as if we had stepped
    over the edge
        of good taste
            onto a strange peninsula

remote beyond all reckoning
    where for three days
        and nights we went further
            and further into each other

and we did not turn back,
    we did not turn away.
        It was not a Revival meeting
            or a snake handling ceremony

but I'm not ashamed to say
    in that dingy room
        on the edge of nowhere
            I learned to pray, to become

a fundamentalist of your body.
       I don't know if I
              was lost or saved,
                     but it was there, love,

I felt an angel's possessing
       grip, the flames
              rising from your skin,
                     the shadow of the divine.

I knelt in a pentecostal church
       and spoke in tongues
              before I was lifted up
                     and carried into the light.

Husband and Wife

I woke up and found you above me—
your face peering down through shadows,
your hair sweeping slowly across my chest,
your voice crying out a name in the darkness,
my name, just once,
as if it had been pulled out of you
from a great distance, from oblivion itself,
as if a rib had been carved from my side
and given back in your shape,
as if we were two halves of one body—
a cell, an egg floating in water,
a new being gathering force like a storm
(wind tossed, tossing the wind)
until the rain seeding the clouds
and the thunder bloating the sky
could stand it no longer
and we burst forth in a wild flood.

2

Then we were falling away from each other,
breaking apart, tearing ourselves loose
from a cupped palm
and putting on our torsos, our limbs,
our separate distinguishable selves.
The ecstasy—the oneness—was unbearable
and so we expelled ourselves,
who had tasted the fruit,
who had discovered our nakedness . . .
I woke up and found you lying next to me,
already awake. How long did we stay there
like strangers, shoulder to shoulder,
scarcely touching, until you got up
and went to the window, and I followed?
Outside, the branches scraped in the garden.
The lightning splitting through the trees
was a sword over Eden's gate.

2

ON LOVE

Prologue

*I woke up to voices speaking of love,
always leading me forward, leading me on,
taking me from the bedroom to the study
in the early morning or late at night,
emanations that seemed to come from night
itself, from leaves opening in the study
where many lives flow together as one
life, my own, these ventures in love.*

Denis Diderot

The strange, enlightening subject of love
creates its own universe of discourse,
which is the least susceptible to reason.
My colleague d'Alembert dreams always
of mathematical formulas, finding ways
to treat subjects with absolute reason
in a precise hierarchy of discourse,
and yet he is unprepared for love—

a subject which seems highly illogical.
One might even say that to embrace Eros
is to enter into a state of visionary
impetuousness with another human being.
D'Alembert suspects that I am being
petulant in my idea of the visionary
dimensions of what we think of as Eros;
he is skeptical of anything illogical

or involuntary, anything beyond reason,
and there is nothing beyond or past love
for no one in the world can explain why
it comes and goes of its own free will.
Eros is not subject to Rational Will
and it pains me that nobody knows why
the crooked course of people in love
can be acutely cruel beyond all reason.

Adam and Eve at the sacred beginning
stand as the first principle of love:
I have dreamt of Eros between equals—

warm-hearted, affectionate, appreciative
(I love you, and therefore I appreciate
our companionship as natural equals).
This serves as an introduction to love,
but only an entry, only a beginning;

for no greater wonder exists than love,
a brutal and creative human discovery.
I conceive desire—sexual love—as Eros,
and passion as the knowledge we embody:
an activity of mind as well as body.
For all those who have experienced Eros,
may these revelations help you discover
yourself the encyclopedia of love.

Giacomo Leopardi

Poetry Would Be a Way of Praising God if God Existed

Deep in the heart of night
I stood on a hill in wintertime
and stared up at the baleful moon.
I was terrified of finding myself
in the midst of nothing, myself
nothingness clarified, like the moon.
I was suffocating inside time,
contemplating the empty night

when a bell rang in the distance
three times, like a heart beating
in the farthest reaches of the sky.
The music was saturated with stillness.
I stood listening to that stillness
until it seemed to fill the sky.
The moon was like a heart beating
somewhere far off in the distance.

But there is no heart in a universe
of dying planets, infinite starry spaces.
Death alone is the true mother of Eros
and only love can revivify the earth,
for what is this emptiness, the earth,
but a black sea pulsing without Eros
under infinitely dead starry spaces?
Love alone can redeem our universe.

Heinrich Heine

I come to you as a whole-hearted man.
I have had myself carried here today
on what we may call my mattress-grave
where I have been entombed for years
(forgive me if I don't stand up this time)
to speculate about the nature of love.

As a cripple talking about physical love,
a subject I've been giving up for years,
I know that my situation (this time
he's gone too far!) is comical and grave.
But don't I still appear to be a man?
Hath not a Jew eyes, etc., at least today?

I am an addict of the human comedy
and I admit every pleasure, especially love,
is like the marriage of the French and Germans
or the eternal quarrel between Space and Time.
We are all creeping madly toward the grave
or leaping forward across the years

(Me, I haven't been able to leap in years)
and bowing under the fiendish blows of Time.
All that can distract us—gentlemen, ladies—
is the splendid warfare between men and women.
I don't hesitate to call the struggle "love."
Look at me: my feverish body is a grave,

I've been living so long on a mattress-grave
that I scarcely even resemble a man,
but what keeps me going is the quest for love.
I may be a dog who has had his day
(admittedly a day that has lasted for years)
but I'm also a formidable intellect of our time

and I'm telling you nothing can redeem Time
or the evident oblivions of the grave
or the crippling paralysis of the years
except the usual enchantments of love.
That's why the night hungers for the day
and the gods—heaven help us—envy the human.

For man and woman, the days pass into years
and the body is a grave filled with time.
We are drowning. All that rescues us is love.

Charles Baudelaire

These speculations afford me great pleasure
beyond human hypocrisy. My subject is love
and my proposition a simple one: erotic love,
which is, after all, a fatal form of pleasure,
resembles a surgical operation, or torture.
Forgive me if I sound ironic or cynical
but, I'm certain you'll agree, cynicism
is sometimes needed in discussing torture.

Act One, Scene One: The score is "Love."
The setting of a great operatic passion.
At first the lovers have equal passion
but, it turns out, one always seems to love
the other less. He, or she, is the surgeon
applying a scalpel to the patient, the victim.
I know because I have been that victim;
I have also been the torturer, the surgeon.

Can you hear those loud spasmodic sighs?
Who hasn't uttered them in hours of love?
Who hasn't drawn them from his (or her) lover?
It's sacrilegious to call such noises "ecstasies"
when they're a species of decomposition,
surrendering to death. We can get drunk
on each other, but don't pretend being drunk
puts us in a sudden death-defying position.

Why are people so proud of that spellbound
look, that hard stiffening between the legs?
Example One: She ran her hand down my legs

until I felt I'd been gagged and bound.
Example Two: She no longer gave me pleasure,
nonetheless, I rested my hand on her nude body
casually, I leaned over and tasted her body
until her whole being trembled with pleasure.

The erotic is an intimate form of cruelty
and every pleasure can be used to prostitute
another: I love you and become your prostitute
but my generosity is your voluptuous cruelty.
Sex is humiliation, a terrifying game
in which one partner loses self-control.
The subject concerns ownership or control
and that makes it an irresistible game.

I once heard the question discussed:
Wherein consists love's greatest pleasure?
I pondered the topic with great pleasure
but the whole debate filled me with disgust.
Someone declared, *We love a higher power.*
Someone said, *Giving is better than receiving,*
though someone else retorted, *I prefer receiving.*
No one there ever connected love to power.

Someone truly announced, *The greatest pleasure
in love is to populate the State with children.*
But must we really be no better than children
whenever we discuss the topic of pleasure?
Pain, I say, is inseparable from pleasure
and love is but an exquisite form of torture.
You need me, but I carry the torch for her ...
Evil comes enswathed in every pleasure.

Margaret Fuller

Thank you for attending this conversation on love.
I am going to argue in the Nineteenth Century
a woman can no longer be sacrificed for love.
The Middle Ages are over, ladies and gentlemen,

and I am going to argue in the Nineteenth Century
we are not merely wives, whores, and mothers.
The Middle Ages are over, ladies. And gentlemen,
we can now be sea captains, if you will.

We are not merely wives, whores, and mothers.
We can be lawyers, doctors, journalists,
we can now be sea captains, if you will.
What matters to us is our own fulfillment.

We can be lawyers, doctors, journalists
who write ourselves into the official scripts.
What matters to us is our own fulfillment.
It is time for Eurydice to call for Orpheus

and to sing herself into the official scripts.
She is no longer a stranger to her inheritance.
It is time for Eurydice to call for Orpheus
and to move the earth with her triumphant song.

She is no longer a stranger to her inheritance.
She, too, feels divinity within her body
and moves the earth with her triumphant song.
God created us for the purpose of happiness.

She, too, feels divinity within her body.
Our holiest work is to transform the earth.
God created us for the purpose of happiness.
The earth itself becomes a parcel of heaven.

Our holiest work is to transform the earth.
Thank you for attending this conversation on love.
The earth itself becomes a parcel of heaven.
A woman can no longer be sacrificed for love.

Ralph Waldo Emerson

Let's devour the blessed apple of love.
I have been told that in public discourse
my true reverence for intellectual discourse
has made me indifferent to the subject of love,
but I almost shrink at such disparaging words
since I believe love created the world.
What else, after all, perpetuates the world
except enacted love? I savor the words.

The study of love is a question of facts
and a matter of dreams, a dream that matters.
Lovers are scientists studying heavenly matters
while their bodies connect the sweetest facts.
Please don't blush when I speak of love
as the reunion of two independent souls
who have drifted since birth as lost souls
but now come together in eternal love.

There can be no love without natural sympathy.
Let's say you're a hunter who excels at business
(I'm aware this may be none of my business)
but for me it doesn't arouse much sympathy.
Let's say, however, you drink tea in the morning
and like to eat apple pie for breakfast;
we both walk through the country very fast
watching the darkness turn into early morning

and this creates a mutual bond between us
that leads to a soulful sharing of sabbaths.
The heart has its jubilees and sabbaths

when a fiery lightning strikes between us.
I do not shy away from the subject of sex
which is, after all, a principle of the universe
(it is also, alas, a principle of my verse)
since we are bound to each other through sex.

Look how the girls flirt with the boys
while the boys slowly encircle the girls.
The village shops are crowded with girls
lingering over nothing, to talk with boys.
Romance is the beginning of celestial ecstasy,
an immortal hilarity, a condition of joy:
civilization itself depends on the joy
of standing beside ourselves with ecstasy.

Love is a bright foreigner, a foreign self
that must recognize me for what I truly am;
only my lover can understand me as I am
when I am struggling to create myself.
So, too, I must love you as you truly are—
but what is that? Under your cool visage
and coy exterior, your advancing age,
I sense the young passion of who you are.

The lover comes with something to declare—
such declarations affirm the nature of love.
Here is what the lover says to his love
in the heat of passion, this I declare:
My love for you is a voluptuous world
where the seasons appear as a bright feast.
We can sit together at this delicious feast.
Come lie down with me and devour the world.

George Meredith

The ordeal of modern love forms my subject—
but what else could it form? The naked rage
and enraged nakedness of people in marriage
is not an uplifting or even elevated subject,
though no doubt worthy of our attention
to scrutinize how a durable dual alliance
becomes a nightmarish fatal misalliance
with some attentiveness, some inattention.
It takes no time at all—or a lifetime—
to exchange a companion—a corporal mate—
for one with whom you're no longer intimate,
even if Eros lasts a supposed lifetime.
I once imagined wedded bliss as sacred,
but marriage as the outcome of romantic love
encourages the expiration of romantic love,
leaving behind a breathless shell: the sacred.

What a spectacle! Remember those early days—
infatuated, free—when I was so smitten
with you (but were you ever so smitten
with me?—I think not), ever in a daze
over your round handsome face and blond hair
parted down the middle, your sardonic brow
(I did like it when you arched an eyebrow),
your lithe body that seemed to glide on air.
You could knit a group with a cunning wit,
talk the talk of the very smartest men,
speak with your fingers, make me a man,
break up a party with your scapular wit.
I proposed marriage for the seventh time—
once in a boat, once in a languishing garden
after a heavy storm that had shocked the garden—
before you agreed to accept me for all time.

Pause for our courtship, which was delicious,
the night your daughter surprised us in a kiss
("Mother, I can't bear that man!"), our kiss
after the wedding at St. George's (also delicious),
our honeymoon in the Rhineland and in France
where you opened the wild floodgates to yourself
for the first time. (Remember calling yourself
Citoyenne de la Grande Republique de France?)
But at home we discovered our grave mistake.
You were nine years senior and wanted comfort,
but I simply refused to supply that comfort
by accepting any job that would be a mistake.
I was never a Peacock strolling through life,
strutting my feathers. I was not your father,
refused the temptation to become your father:
you scorned my pen, your lodgings, our life.

The snake enters the garden as Henry Wallis,
who painted Mary into a *Fireside Reverie*
(one imagines the nature of *his* reverie).
Look up *The Death of Chatteron* by H. Wallis
and you'll find me as a model for the poet.
Hah! He had another way of murdering me,
unleashing my wife's melancholy anger at me
for trying to exist in the world as a poet.
One night I was awakened by steady crying.
I turned over, found her wracked by sobs,
but how had I managed to cause such sobs?
Come here, dearest. Why are you crying?
Let me wipe away these salty blue tears.
I cannot fathom the excess of this sadness
that brims our cup with overflowing sadness:
tell me what is flooding you with tears.

That was when she resorted again to tears,
admitting freely she had taken a lover
to replace me. O my wild faithless love,
even now it leaves me sorely bereft, tears
me to pieces recalling how I, too, would cry
and shake with fear, fury, even remorse
(but why should *I* be filled with remorse?)
until I was too exhausted even to cry
or to reproach you with what you had done
to me, to yourself, to our unsullied love.
Could I ever think it unsullied, love,
or were all our years together now undone
save what existed—did not exist—between us?
Why had the fretful serpent roiled the garden
and slithered into our lodge, our poor den?
I could not comprehend what happened to us.

I would have slept like an overtired child,
but you decided it was the hour to admit,
to confess, bravely to confess, to admit
(*spew it out!*) you were having a child
(*there, it's said!*) and it was not mine.
I reeled and scarcely knew where to turn,
I sat down, stood up, left and returned,
almost convinced myself that it was mine,
that it could never belong to anyone else,
though of course that was quite impossible . . .
Suddenly everything had become impossible
because you had changed into someone else
whom I could not recognize, did not know.
What poison jealousies had swallowed us, love,
since we were three—husband, wife, lover?
I swooned at a faithlessness I could not know.

Then came the wretched black days of agony
that turn into weeks dissolving into months.
Has it really been two—three—four months
we have endured this unendurable agony?
There are considerate days when we console
each other for the sorrows come to pass,
endless days that never seem to pass,
days when we are truly lost, inconsolable . . .
Some nights we cannot bear to be apart,
others we cannot bear to stay together.
How are we to keep the child together?
We'll stay at home, no, we'll live apart . . .
But if you leave me, if you run off again
to your adultery, world without recall
(for I had drawn the sword that severs all),
my dearest, I vow never to see you again . . .

That was the ending, what had befallen,
what we could not forget, never forgive.
I kept your son who also could not forgive
you for abandoning him, for having fallen.
You could depart to Capri with Mr. Wallis—
we would have memories, debts, loneliness.
What matter if I perish from loneliness
I would never take you back from Wallis,
I would die before I looked you in the eyes
ever again, who had proved me so tame,
who viewed me as a beast she longed to tame.
It's dead. But nights, when I close my eyes,
I discover you standing before me, love,
my steadfast warrior, my maddest maiden
who once had given me the peace of Eden,
my one desire, my faithless modern love.

Lafcadio Hearn

I, too, must make diverse pilgrimages,
but every now and then I need to pause
and take a moment *to sound my barbaric*
yawp over the rooftops of the world.
I have tramped across much of the world
in search of the exotic, the "barbaric,"
but some nights I linger and pause
to celebrate another type of "pilgrimage"

to a holy shrine nestling in black waters
and black hills striped with moonlight.
I am speaking of Creole love, a dark
Venus; the attraction of heavenly bodies;
the momentum of two planets, two bodies
orbiting together in a magnetic dark
that resounds in the spheres like light
moving over the dim face of the waters.

I shall honor the darker style of Eros.
Admittedly, white beauty inspires awe
like a snowy statue, but darker beauty
instigates passion. Men might pray
to a fair goddess who tramples prayer,
but I prefer the softer eye of beauty
encouraging affection instead of awe.
All the most famous canticles of Eros

have been devoted to tinted daughters,
praising the deeper shades of beauty:
bronze-red, copper-brown, olive-black . . .

The greatest love song is Solomon's song
of the Shulamite—the Song of Songs—
and the Shulamite was a richly black,
indeed, a notoriously colored beauty:
I am black but beautiful, O ye daughters

of Jerusalem ... Listen to the Laureate
promise: *I will take some savage woman*
[and] *she shall bear my dusky race* ...
Just so. I, too, shall take a woman
many will despise, an intoxicating woman
who mixes the blood of different races,
for I love the mulatto "Ethiopian" woman
who hypnotizes me into a voodoo state.

I should declare myself as a hybrid:
I was born on a southern Ionian island,
delivered from a cold Anglo-Irish father
and a fiery, passionate Greek mother
(everything good in me comes from Mother,
everything compromised from Father)
who named me "Lafcadio" after an island;—
thus the soul in me is natively hybrid.

I am also fond of the idea—the truth—
that there is no such thing as a pure
specimen;—we are like a blood broth
with lots of ingredients for a heritage.
There *are* no white people, no parentage
is clear for those stirred into the broth,
though some pretend to be racially "pure"
because they cannot bear the bloody truth.

The idea of culture: *creolize civilization!*
Of course, I also adore the "Orient,"
and soon I will be leaving for Japan;—
perhaps when I am there I should arrange
to marry, or let a marriage be arranged
with a country-woman from ancient Japan;—
together we could found a United Orient
against this barbarous Western civilization.

Now I'd like to sanctify human happiness
by listening to the music of Creoles;—
a vital, obstinate, proud, mongrel music
that makes you hold each other and sway . . .
(I do love a body that can hold sway
over me with a supple-shadowed music.)
Naturally, the food of love is Creole;—
I welcome you to a shocking happiness.

Oscar Wilde

To set the scene: we're in a country house
with cool lily ponds and scented rose gardens,
gay herbaceous flowers and strolling peacocks.
It should be evident I'm one of those peacocks—
an overdressed lecturer strutting through gardens,
while you're the audience who brings down the house.

I address the well-dressed features of love—
its silliness, grandeur, outlandish bondage—
since I'm the speaker wearing a fur-lined coat.
(I hope you admire this heliotropic waistcoat.)
Still, now that I've reached a certain "age"
I'd rather walk naked in the name of love

like my beloved Greeks, who were truly modern.
Every great love is a full-fledged tragedy
with a lot of corpses littering the stage.
In the end, order is restored to the stage
but that scarcely mitigates a personal tragedy.
I suppose this viewpoint is "absolutely modern":

love is an unruly and subversive passion.
It is exquisite, mixing ardour and indifference.
It is moody, sacrificial, storied, delicious.
Of course, a forbidden affair is most delicious
(think of Adam and Eve, with a divine difference)
because we give ourselves to unholy passion.

I am eager to confess vermillion love for him
and I will never surrender sex to my country.
Put a true poet in prison for loving boys
and—voilà—he will continue loving boys
just as a patriot doesn't deny his country,
no matter how commonly it disappoints him.

Now I speak of love that dares not speak
its name, and I will not be silenced;
I shall never be shamed by this affection.
It is a spiritual—a physical—affection,
a Platonic voice ringing out the silence,
a Shakespearean sonnet that needs to speak:

Let me not to the marriage of true minds
Admit impediments; love is not love
Which alters when it alteration finds.
I am astonished by what your manner finds
working in me, inflaming the idea of love,
enlarging our bodies by engaging our minds.

The gods are strange. They brew us fatal
pleasures, they use our virtues to betray us,
they break our wings across the wheel of loving.
Yet I cannot—I will not—relinquish loving
the distant star that seems destined for us,
though our bodies are sullied, our desires fatal.

Love is not unnatural, though it may be wild.
I imagine a canonization of true feeling,
of freedom, such as defined the saints.
You may consider it odd to speak of saints
but I understand their martyrdom of feeling.
Think of love when you think of Oscar Wilde.

Tristan Tzara

There is no such thing as a dada lecture
a manifesto is addressed to the whole world
I am opposed to every system except one
love is irrational and you are the reason

a manifesto is addressed to the whole world
but bells ring out for no reason at all
love is irrational and you are the reason
I am a bridge harboring your darkness

but bells ring out for no reason at all
you are a fresh wind assaulted by sails
I am a bridge harboring your darkness
let's not lash ourselves to the flagpoles

you are a fresh wind assaulted by sails
I am a wound that sprays your salt
let's not lash ourselves to the flagpoles
let's not swim to the music of sailors

I am a wound that sprays your salt
ambassadors of sentiment hate our chorus
let's not swim to the music of sailors
we cast our anchors into the distance

ambassadors of sentiment hate our chorus
they can't pollute our smokiest feelings
we cast our anchors into the distance
we sail our boats for the netherworld

they can't pollute our smokiest feelings
each of us has a thousand virginities
we sail our boats for the netherworld
I'm giving you all my nothingness

each of us has a thousand virginities
we still consider ourselves charming
I'm giving you all my nothingness
I have doubted everything but this

we still consider ourselves charming
there is no such thing as a dada lecture
I have doubted everything but this
I am opposed to every system except one

Guillaume Apollinaire

It's the right time to pollinate the air
And speak to you with an unpolished accent
About the terrible war-like god of love
Swaggering through the muddy trenches of love-
Lessness just to hunt down a bloody scent
In the open heart of Guillaume Apollinaire

A count without money a real no account
Wandering aimlessly through the Paris streets
From dawn until dusk lusting and listing
Like a wounded soldier who keeps reenlisting
Long after the war has ended in the streets
I followed you so often that I lost count

Of the nights that mean the most to love
Sweet tender pornographic and passionate
What comes reeling back is how the light-
Ning flashed over the rooftops at twilight
And we clung together frightened and passionate
Until we came apart in the soggy arms of love

Eros and Thanatos are like eternal twins
Smutty brothers volunteering for the front
Where I smelled the shameless odor of death
And dreamt of your nude body *le petit mort*
Rising up in me like a sudden affront
My lightning my beloved my despondent twin

When I think of my sexual midadventures
With women who were flares and faulty wires
A cubist a governess a teacher a redhead
I remember peering into an X-ray of my head
And seeing a labyrinth of crossed wires
That corresponded to my erotic adventures

But when I'm having nightmares about the War
And the shrapnel lodged inside my skull
Your face alone comes brimming into mind
Like the sun itself and I scarcely mind
You've moved to the inside of my skull
Bandaged securely by the Great War

Sit down with a drink of cointreau or whiskey
Stand up and erect for once a Pole in air
I have something to tell you about kindness
The adored food of love is milky kindness
I may not have become Apollo inerrant
Or anything French but poor Kostrowitzky

A bastard zone of uncertainty a Polish nomad
A clowning criminal drunk critic Orphic sickness
Who oscillates between adventure and order
A lieutenant giving a mortal commanding order
A man who sees life as an exultant sickness
A tragic surrealist driving people mad

But at least I recognized the bright flames
Of your hair and your funny scowling lips
And your eyes that looked clear through me
And your scarred hands that will soon bury me
Promise you'll wear a song upon your lips
Come down to find me singing in the flames

Milena Jesenská

I am raising my voice in a tribute to love.
I present myself to you as a Czech journalist
and translator—and also as a modern woman
who has recognized the cruelty of our century.
Thus far it has been a calamitous century;
I haven't lost my vital optimism as a woman
or my curiosity as a practicing journalist,
but now my voice is an obituary for love

because Franz Kafka—the writer—has died.
He was a master of the alienated sentence,
a Jew, a jackdaw, a cauldron of anxiety,
a crisis masquerading as a human body.
He never should have entertained a body
since it caused him overwhelming anxiety
which he transformed into a guilty sentence
that turned on itself and would never die.

Kafka saw a strange and terrifying world
filled with invisible wingbeats and demons.
He suffered for years from a lung disease
which he also encouraged by his thinking.
He had his own gruesome way of thinking
about the dark receptivity of his disease:
he viewed his lungs as a cradle for demons
who would tear apart and destroy his world.

I suspect he was too vulnerable to live,
too kind to fight. He had a frightening
delicacy, an uncompromising refinement.

Few people ever knew him as a human being
because he was such an odd, solitary being.
The books he wrote have great refinement—
I find them stark, funny, and frightening.
Is it possible he knew too much to live?

He had nothing to do with earthly business—
strangeness came through everything he said.
For him money, typewriters, foreign exchange
were mysterious secrets, mystical things.
He tended to overestimate practical things
he couldn't cope with, manage, or change.
Thus he admired his fiancée, so he said,
because she was very "good at business"

and therefore a true person of the world.
When I told him about my husband, Ernst,
who was unfaithful to me a hundred times,
his face lit up with genuine amazement.
It was the same awe—the same amazement—
he felt for conductors who know the times
of all the trains. He was completely earnest
in his respect for those who run the world.

He was a naked man trying to live alone
in a universe where everyone was dressed.
He had no refuge from the elements, exposed
to those things from which we are protected.
He was lost because he was unprotected,
a human negative who had been exposed.
I supposed his terror could be addressed,
but night was a blankness he faced alone.

No sanatorium could possibly cure him
because he never recovered from his fear
of living like an insignificant cockroach
sacrificed on the altar of the abnormal.
But what if we are sick and he was normal?
He perceived the courage of the cockroach
who crawls in the dust and encounters fear.
The darkness was a mirror reflecting him.

I admit I needed him. I tried to help,
but my love turned into one more catastrophe.
I have his letters, diaries, stories
that scrutinize an inscrutable disaster.
Maybe his character *was* a human disaster,
but he paid for it with uncanny stories
which will survive the coming catastrophe.
And now we must live without his help.

D. H. Lawrence

A Short History of Love

After the sweet red wine and the dry lecture,
"The History of Love in Western Imagination"
(history is loveless without imagination)
we could not abide another listless lecture

and so we slipped into the castle library
and pushed highbacked chairs against a door
that refused to lock (so jam the door!)
and knelt to each other in the library.

I confess my fear of patrolling watchmen;
you seemed courageous and sure, as always:
I have learned to adore your myriad ways
of taking us back into man and woman . . .

And when we lay naked among the books,
the bookshelves enclosed a sacred garden
for Adam and Eve safely restored to Eden,
ourselves immersed in a paradise of books.

H. D.

Do not blame Helen
for starting these wars
between men, and
do not indict
Aphrodite
holding in her hand
a helmet of Mars.
Helen:

my mother's name,
the Muse, the creator,
the memory in all women
of all ages
who are hostages
to paternal men,
the phallic creator
I shall not name.

I would be Hermes,
a winged messenger
bringing you a scroll
of enchantments
against disenchantments—
the slashed scroll—
of Time, a messenger
at war with Hermes.

So arise and face me,
Priapus, with beautiful horns—
I break off a branch
of the priestess,
the mythical priestess
whose spear, a branch,
will bind your horns
in homage to me.

Egypt in bondage,
Egypt in love,
the thousand-petalled lily,
a hieroglyph on the wall,
a fiery sign on the wall
of the ritual red lily,
a form of love
adept against bondage.

So we begin again
and sail in ecstasy
to the womb-like sun,
the oracular image,
the radiant image
of the awakening sun
rising in ecstasy
for us, merging again.

Federico García Lorca

I would invite loneliness into the room
as a tutelary spirit, a sure remembrance
of the scared blue child in every listener.
I beg the simple promise of your attention
as I imagine a sign that says *Only Mystery*
above the entrance. I invoke this mystery,
even as I summon a moment of pure attention
(improvising in the presence of each listener),
for nothing is accomplished without remembrance . . .
Solitude has now been welcomed into the room.

I will try not to exhaust you with proofs
that Morpheus—mustached old man—would enjoy.
Whoever says, "I love, I want," knows everything
about the obscure longings of the night:
what bulls desire, what barren women desire,
what goats, princesses, orange trees desire . . .
The lover who exposes his chest to the night
recognizes how death nestles in everything
wounded, but can never assassinate joy:
I offer my body as the naked Spanish proof.

Love is a benediction, an ache, a dark need
that dizzies us with its demands, desires,
Oriental fulfillments, fantasies, fairy tales . . .
I myself was formed by a dream of gardens:
throbbing irises and peonies, swooning roses.
Outside, I appeared as one of those roses,
but inside I was a lily of the garden,
impossible to water. I made up fairy tales
and puppet plays to enact my budding desires,
for I could never be just the one I'd need.

I first tasted the pink pill of unhappy love
as a child—O it was painful to swallow!
After that, I was poisoned many more times
but survived—a Gypsy Job—to tell the tale
in ballads made from love and renunciation,
in romances, laments, lyrics of renunciation
and longing, telluric tragedies, inverted tales
of blood feuds—blood weddings!—of distant times
all too familiar, far too bitter to swallow:
must we destroy what we can or cannot love?

To burn with red desire is the open road
(an ode to Walt Whitman), but to keep silent
is a punishment we bring upon ourselves.
The thwarted rose becomes a dying thorn,
uncrowned, in the left side of the rosebed,
but when we water love in our soiled bed
we carve away the strangling black thorn
and bloom into our bright celestial selves
where, for a moment, even death is silent,
homesick for our crooked, eternal road . . .

But two is a number of harsh separation,
a wall built around someone else's shadow
(a shadow dissolving on someone else's wall).
I want to be more than a wish for death
flying through voices, guitars, trees, beds.
Let waterfalls wash over their own beds
and rivers open their loud mouths to death,
I will throw my damp torso against the wall
in order to penetrate your smoky shadow
supine under a crescent of separation.

How much love can we cast off, or waste,
craving to dissect each other like light?
When I consider it calmly, I don't know if
it's so fortuitous for a sewing machine
to meet an umbrella on a dissecting table—
who could embrace on a surgeon's table?
Wouldn't it be better if the toothy machine
met the cloudy umbrella in a garden or, if
you prefer, in a field galloping with moonlight
where I sewed your umbrella around my waist?

Spain has blackened herself into a mother
fanatic to devour the poor like animals.
She carries a chastity belt for virgins,
a knotted rope for the backs of young boys,
and conducts her inquisitions every night;
but I want to escape those sterile nights
into the feverish world we created as boys
acting like cocks, tomcats, purring virgins,
fig-trees snaking across the garden, animals
rolling under the surveillance of the mother . . .

But you never step into the same past twice,
or hear the identical lecture, or undress
the same lover; you wear another body.
Each of us harbors a fugitive, an outcast;
whatever stone I may cast at the stranger,
I soon discover nothing could be stranger
than my own fluctuating heart, downcast
and jubilant in pursuit of a human body
to encounter and woo, to sing and undress;
the same soul never steps into the river twice.

Take these fiery kisses into your hands.
Go, search, stumble, agitate, and live,
but remember our wild erotic hallelujahs,
nights we ate the lilies, drank the roses,
transformed our bodies into church bells
that towered over high cathedral bells,
even as we scorched our lips on rosaries.
Our solitudes have met in erotic hallelujahs
that prey upon us, praying that we live.
The mystery of Eros burns in our hands.

Robert Desnos

I would like to crack open my heart for you
and offer the dreaming voice of Robert Desnos
a friend who goes into a trance for love
an automatic swoon speaking surrealist love
an epic adventure in the voice of Robert Desnos
eagerly sleepwalking his open heart for you

telling your fortune which is always good
how fine-looking and well-dressed you are
just like my beloved my planetary star-
fish swimming with the other fishy stars
in watery constellations wherever you are
I will find you because our love is good

I wondered if I was capable of surprising you
embracing you with desire for Eros it's life
going down to the casino to take a chance
by throwing the dice for love for chance
for giving Eros another chance *Rrose Sélavy*
I've always had a weakness for surprising you

with gambling shadows miscellaneous dreams
voyaging to the bottom of the forest the sea
where we can wander like derelict ships
wrecking ourselves the other obedient ships
riding sea-horses directly out of the sea
into the night and its panoply of dreams

ROBERT DESNOS

I never loved any school system except you
my unconscious my newsprint my black film
I was the poorest student talkative dis-
organized scatter-brained inattentive dis-
obedient lazy until I learned of *film noir*
reading the mysterious script of you

I foretold arms leaning on barbed wire fences
transports leading nowhere without walls
against the spirit of resistance concentration
camps where I will never lose concentration
because I will fly to you beyond the walls
embracing our future misfortune beyond fences

I have dreamt of your love so far so long
in every séance in every lecture on love
I'm certain I shall find you someday
in the corner seat of night the first day
you've wandered into a lecture on love
dear I've been waiting for you so long

I would like to crack open my heart for you
my desire my destiny of furious shadows
drunken kisses ecstatic blue mirage
the hour of miracles dawns in every age
I waken to the shadow of your shadows.
I return to the waking world for you

Gertrude Stein

Love happens to be an astonishing state,
a state in which all of us are astonished.

Everyone asks questions of this state
and then the state asks questions of everyone.

It's a country with a queer feeling
for the state, no apologies are necessary.

I should not neglect hapless exchanges:
what does she mean by laughing at me?

I should not neglect secrets and dungeons,
mistakes, confessions in tears at midnight.

Anger is pungent, but forgiveness is sweet.
I never knew this fruit until I tasted it.

It's infamous. We never trusted the garden
until we were expelled from it, together.

The pink melon has the flavor of joy,
but you must peel it, deliciously.

I like to be seized here and here.
Touch me again, my spoiled pugilist.

I was aghast at your red houseslippers,
but I admit to adoring your feet.

Don't deny it. For a time we were plagued
by baby-talk, toothlessness, bonbons.

We recovered nicely, my dark magic.
You are a hat pulled out of my rabbit.

Did I mention gaiety, fancy summer balls,
your blue dress with exquisite buttons?

I like it when we eat on moving trains.
The food slides a little under our manners.

We came home and cleaned the closets.
Look at these natty stockings. Rip!

We laughed until our sides split.
We split until our sides laughed.

Once, we were so annoyed by newspapers
we blamed each other for being sick.

The slamming door can be lonesome.
Some aloneness. The door slamming.

Adverse to verse, I added verses,
stanzas against her shackles. Versus.

She pruned my puns. I smoked and fumed.
How lousy to be jealous. The sweet louse.

Since when do plants know our names:
love-in-a mist, love-lies-bleeding.

It's dangerous out there in the tropics.
Would you like some tea? Kisses. More.

A lice had lice, and the lice had Alice.
The parlor was atrocious. How lascivious.

So I am splashed again by paintings:
your colorful looks make me giddy.

We are pleased by our great fortune.
In the midst of our fortune we are pleased.

You are my passport to a lovely estate.
I have something stately to declare.

Not surprising I like to make sentences.
The sentences themselves are surprised.

I'd like to know if happiness is
a sentence, a question, or an exclamation.

All of us are astonished by love.
Love happens to be. An astonishing state.

Dr. X

So let's create a scene: I'm "in love"—
that is to say, a little lost and desperate,
nervous, alert, excited, no, thrilled to be
entering into such an exalted state of be-
ing with so many irrational and desperate
feelings attached to it, all labelled "love,"

some that make me unfamiliar to everyone,
especially myself. Who is this capricious
stranger sending birds-of-paradise on a whim
(I usually consider flowers a vulgar whim)
or skipping out of work on the capricious
hope you'll drop everything and everyone

and join me for a stroll along the beach
and a romp in the sand? It's cold,
but I'll bring sweaters and a warm blanket
so that we can snuggle up in the blanket
and marshal our bodies to defeat the cold.
To hell with the officer patrolling the beach!

Let's try to regress a little as we walk.
Feet and hands. Your mouth upon my mouth.
The sturdy wooden fence where as a child
I was separated from the other children
and felt the fog swallowing me like a mouth
and the loud waves roaring up the walk.

DR. X

Come closer, squeeze my hand, hold me
so that I can replace the childish dark
with wine-filled moonlight and two bodies
turning themselves into a single body
reclining nervously in an adolescent dark.
Who is this stranger kneeling beside me?

The unconscious exists. We enter its depths
through dreaming Eros—another person:
a tart caress, a bone-ache, a yearning call
to be drowned and saved, lost and recalled
from our identities as a daughter, a son,
two children swimming through murky depths

toward father fear, mother milk, the waters
where we will comply with nothing again
but our own memories, fantasies, interior
spaces, softening shells, oceanic interior . . .
We are shaped and reshaped yet again
in the wavering white body of these waters

where we keep flowing and flooding back
through a narrow channel, fishy waters,
still moved to be moving past common sense,
a giddy blue vertigo, pleasurable descents
into the touching darkness of these waters
slipping farther down, even farther back . . .

One moment we are entangled in the sand,
wrapped inside a blanket, inside each other,
the next we are falling through the waves
into another sandbar, another wave of waves
where we are sliding right through each other
to an unknown bottom floating under sand.

69

It's eerie down here just swimming around.
Where am I now? And what have I become?
Have I sunk to the dregs, the very pit?
I feel I'm the fruit itself, the pit
inside the fruit. Can you taste me? Come:
I am salty, porous, tentacular, round.

Milk me. Feed me back to my own birth.
I am an infant carried back down into
the milky ways of the maternal breast,
bobbing up, swelling on the sea's breast.
Infinitesimal. Content to be crawling into
every silence I have lost since birth.

I feel drowsy in the wet nub of sleep,
but now something resumes again in me,
wild, spermatic, explosive, dark.
I am a serpent hissing in the dark,
wriggling into the cave in you, in me,
which is mad and anarchic—awake, asleep.

And suddenly I am being reeled back,
rudely pulled away. Where have I been?
You are the warmth that carried me there
(wherever it was I was when I was there),
heralds me home from where I have been.
I look into light that comes flooding back.

Just move away from me for a moment:
I crossed a faultline of the body
and can't stop shuddering with ecstasy
or desolation—a desolate ecstasy,
a plenitude falling away from the body,
these laughing tears, forever in a moment.

Come here. I was terrified and calm
before I had a body, a self, or even knew
I shall never be the thing I seek.
But tonight I found what I will seek
in you again, this compensatory know-
ing that left me terrified, made me calm.

And so we become our separate selves,
two people sitting up, brushing off sand.
Such is the candor—the intimacy—of love
that it has given us back original love
and restored us refreshed to human sand.
Eros is our way of re-forming ourselves.

Bertolt Brecht

Let's light a match to the good old days.
I'll just assume you won't mind if I smoke
a cigar or two while blabbing about love,
the most basic and preposterous subject
imaginable. I object to this subject,
since the whole idea of sentimental love
should be going up quickly in thick smoke
like our civilization in the bad news days.

Here's something to shock you: middle class
love is like everything else middle class;
money counts and what it counts—what matters—
is who's on top and who's on the bottom
in the sexual exchange. Don't be an ass:
things will improve when we take matters
out of the greedy paws of the ruling class
that has landed us in such a rich morass

and hold them in our own hands. Good manners,
vague ideas, and false promises about Eros
should not cover up the reality of marriage
based on property rights and bank accounts.
Love must be free and clear on all accounts
to survive the impossible chains of marriage
that have little to do with genuine Eros
and much to do with morals and manners.

What works for you must also work for me.
You don't need to study all of Karl Marx
(though it may help) to learn money affects

everything in modern life, including marriage
(maybe I should say "especially marriage").
We can create our own theatrical effects
in the world, making our sexual marks
by bringing everything down to you and me—

two people, two bodies, on equal terms
before God, the law, history. Come here.
We can't be bought and we won't be sold;
we're becoming our own means of production
(owning, I suppose, means of reproduction)
and thus we will never need to be consoled
for what we've put down—put out—to be here
loving each other simply, on equitable terms.

Romance: a bedroom farce, a mock epic
complete with overcostumed actors swooning
over each other to recite terrible lines—
"I need you," *"Je t'adore,"* "I despise you
and everything shallow and silly about you . . ."
(Thus we go on feeding each other lines.)
Here's a stage where we keep swooning
and cueing each other into the next epoch,

so let's screw. We can't solve the problem
of the Board of Trade in downtown Chicago
that has caused me disappointment and grief
as I have come to understand its miseries,
but we can set our bodies against a series
of abstract horrors, the miserable grief
that would turn us into chattel, human cargo.
Let's really act up—act out—the problem.

Lie down with me on the scummy sidewalks
where we can hear drums beating at night
and rats crawling through dank sewers
under skyscrapers rising at all hours.
Someday this world will be all ours
(or maybe not)—we'll inherit the sewers
and streetlamps, whores working at night
on pockmarked streets, pissy sidewalks.

I won't let bitterness quench my thirst—
and you shouldn't either. We're a chorus,
so let's tip a drink or two to dissolution
and disaffection. We raised the morale
by lowering (and lifting) our own moral
standards, which may not pose a solution
but does contribute to the general chorus
and satisfies a sexual itch and thirst.

Our destiny is freedom. Our free love
may—or may not—give us the true height
needed to live as artists in the world,
but it's our best premise, our last hope.
I suspect we cannot survive without hope
that together we can change the world
a little. It's our longing for height,
our destiny to free ourselves for love.

Marina Tsvetaeva

Human thresholds are meant to be crossed,
so please come in and make yourself at home.
I'm certainly not going to deliver *A Lecture
on Love* (what an insufferable word, "lecture"),
though I shall speak about the essential home-
lessness of love, always star-crossed . . .

I have a talent for "non-reciprocal love"
and all my work is an argument for rapture.
When you love a person you always want him
to disappear so your mind can work on him.
The imagination is a storm-cloud of rapture
which I have scattered, like unhappy love.

"A person has to be condemned to poetry
like a wolf to his howling," A. Bely said,
"but you're a bird that keeps on singing."
I like to be torn apart by my own singing,
like one of Odysseus's men who, it's said,
destroyed himself for the Siren's poetry.

"I have lived with the shudder of longing"
(M. V. wrote), insatiable for the genuine.
I have held a boiling teapot, a frying pan,
a broom, an iron, three babies, and a pen
that stutters with knowledge of the genuine:
I have been hollowed out by sexual longing,

and I've paid for my transcendental passion.
What poet actually *isn't* a Negro, a woman,
or a Jew who has been slain by gentiles?
I know because I've lived among gentiles
as an outcast, a White, an émigré, a woman
despised for her deep and wayward passion.

Admitted: I have been devoured by life—
gathering firewood, feeding my small family.
I have a child who died in an orphanage
(how's that for being "a woman of the age"?)
and I've tried to resurrect my family.
But I've never really cared for "life"—

unmediated, insignificant, all by itself.
Life has to have the plenitude of art.
If I were brought across the sea to Paradise
and forbidden to write, I'd refuse Paradise,
since what good is heaven without art,
which has a joyousness beyond the self?

There are moments in writing like love
when you suddenly set fire to the house
and push your friend from the mountaintop.
They are sublime feelings—the mountaintop
of experience—when you torch the house
and obey the innermost dictates of love.

Wherever you are, I'll reach you, love.
I've named my lust for you "holiness."
We've come to ourselves in a fresh hell
in our century (a godless Russian hell),
but we've also created passionate holiness.
I would be a wing that soars for love.

Zora Neale Hurston

A lot of racial uplifters, "Negrotarians,"
have come to observe one of "The New Negros"
who was rocked in the cradle of Negroism,
talking about love, that universal subject
of speculation. Well, listen up, subject:
I'm here as the "Queen of the Niggerati"
and I don't belong to the school of Negro-
hood sobbing for help from Negrotarians.

I'm black but I'm not "tragically colored"
since I came up in Eatonville, a pure Negro
town without "helpful" southern white folks.
(We weren't the first all-black community—
we *were* the first "incorporated" community.)
I'm fortunate to have studied the folk-
lore and folk-ways of the southern Negro,
crayoning in a book wonderfully colored.

At home I ate the steaming dish of love—
nourishing, plentiful, astoundingly hot.
I thrived on a diet of men and even women
swapping stories—or "lies"—on the porch
of a town store, which was the front porch
of the wide world to me, since those women
and men fed me something astoundingly hot—
spicy tales of life, lessons in love.

I fattened on folk-tales of Brer Rabbit,
Brer Fox, the Devil, Ole Massa and his wife
walking the earth just like the good Lord.
I should have learned one essential lesson
a little better, since it's the basic lesson
of human equality: when the good Lord
sanctifies the union of husband and wife,
it shouldn't be a marriage of fox and rabbit.

Tell that to my first husband who never
wanted me to have a headlong career—
can you imagine? He also taught me
that marriage itself does not make love
or even guarantee anything for lovers . . .
The death of my romantic dream taught me
to become a woman and have a career:
some contracts may not last "forever."

But love when it starts over again
between equals, makes its own sense,
its blossoming trees and aromatic herbs;
it creates its own version of summertime,
an Eden beyond everything, even time,
where we are drenched in God's own herbs
and overwhelmed by the sweetest scents
of forgotten existence remembered again.

The fiend of Hell extends a special gift
to lovers—the slithering serpent of doubt.
I've eaten his apple more than a few times
and it's bitter—I'd just throw it away.
Better to let old Venus have her own way
with you, taking her sweet southern time
to lead you to a Caribbean beyond doubt . . .
Well, listen to me woofing about the gift.

Clothed in mystery henceforth and forever,
love ain't nothing but the easy-going
heart disease, nothing but the journey
to a country from which no one returns
the same. We're pilgrims taking turns
in the holy land, signed up for a journey
to the Mysteries. I, too, shall be going
on this pilgrimage, henceforth and forever.

Oscar Ginsburg

Ladies and Gentlemen, Friends and Strangers:
I stand as a man with spectacles on his nose
(as Isaac Babel said) and autumn in his heart—
a family man, an immigrant, an unknown poet
who scribbles lyrics in the backs of books
about the fair Jerusalem of erotic love.

I never would deliver a commentary on love,
though I affirm its textual strangeness,
a subject taken up by madmen, lovers, poets
who have filled hundreds—thousands—of books
with a Keatsian "holiness of the Heart's
affections," a prayer-book the beloved knows.

Eros is a fiery secret everyone knows
or should know. Cut open my pilgrim heart
and you'll find the sentiments of strangers:
De l'Amour, Liber Amoris, Women in Love,
all the upper registers of romantic poets . . .
(Love, for Jews, is nothing if not bookish.)

A practical woman opened me up like a book
and recited me backwards like a Hebrew poem.
I fell deeply—even desperately—in love
with my wife, a lovely pragmatic stranger
who always wore spectacles on her nose
in matters concerning the human heart.

speak the backward language of my heart:
Reprove a man of sense, and he will love
hee" (Proverbs), and she reproved my books,
ny airiness, my empty purse which—heaven knows—
could never fill for my beloved stranger,
who preferred playing cards to reading poems.

And yet Eros is the surest sword of poets—
drawn across beds, cutting through books.
have known what the migrant heart knows
("O, never say that I was false of heart")
about the steadfast passions of such love
between tender enemies, intimate strangers.

Who knows—but someday the book of my heart
may be inscribed by a stranger, my daughter's
son, brooding about the strangeness of love.

Paul Valéry

My subject is the oddity of amative life.
Most of what has been formulated about love,
frankly, strikes me as euphoric nonsense.
I don't understand my nature, my "essence,"
let alone the essence of the one I love,
and yet my beloved quickens me into life.

Nor do I trust "convictions" or "beliefs"
that suddenly appear like weeds—or obsessions.
Most important thoughts contradict our feelings,
especially when it comes to oceanic feelings
that can turn into a raging sea of obsessions.
And yet I sustain some heartening half-beliefs:

I have actually loved very little in life,
and sometimes in a dream, but I do know
that passion is a mixture of sensual pleasure
and thought itself, the highest pleasure.
It should be a premise that you never know
just who it is you are sleeping with in life

because the object of affection is a phantom.
I think it would be virtually impossible to love
anyone or anything you ever knew completely.
Yet the idea of relinquishing oneself completely
is among the most cherished notions of love.
Does anyone notice that he adores a phantom?

Since I am a foreigner—a mystery—to myself
what is beloved is certain to be unknown.
I love you, and therefore I don't know you.
Hence I'll forge you, I'll even make you
while you unmake yourself, for the unknown
in you is something growing within myself.

Love always moves with a touch of violence
for it is soulful, reckless and inventive.
The purpose of love should be to inspire:
to my mind, to be "in love" means to inspire
someone to be more productive and inventive
with a necessary ache of creative violence.

It is not always good to be—only oneself.
"To fall in love" is to be disturbed by love.
Eros creates a thunderstorm of mad unrest
because the angel of desire demands unrest.
I don't know if it's the acme of shared love,
but caressing another means finding a self.

An excess of the real is a sign of magic,
though I detest easy weeping, and sentimental
displays strike me as a lethal boredom.
Love devises strategies to defeat boredom
and destroys any recourse to the sentimental.
Eros is an affliction that restores magic,

and sexual ferment unleashes a vital energy
which turns into an imaginative urge to work,
for the making of art is our deepest pleasure.
Making love manages to confer such pleasure
on me, an increased consciousness of work.
Ecstasy releases an electrifying energy

that is never fully susceptible to control:
to love is to yield, against one's will,
what was intended exclusively for oneself.
There's madness in liquefying the self
and crossing the threshold of human will,
whereupon the mind seeks to assert control.

Love is an anguished immersion in radiance
comparable to the act of making a poem.
Admittedly, I haven't delivered a speech,
though I have never cared for the speaker's
form: I prefer the struggle to shape a poem.
But I wish you all a form of radiance.

Colette

My mother used to say, "Sit down, dear,
and don't cry. The worst thing for a woman
is her first man—the one who kills you.
After that, marriage becomes a long career."
Poor Sido! She never had another career
and she knew first-hand how love ruins you.
The seducer doesn't care about his woman,
even as he whispers endearments in her ear.

Never let anyone destroy your inner spirit.
Among all the forms of truly absurd courage
the recklessness of young girls is outstanding.
Otherwise there would be far fewer marriages
and even fewer affairs that overwhelm marriages.
Look at me: it's amazing I'm still standing
after what I went through with ridiculous courage.
I was made to suffer, but no one broke my spirit.

Every woman wants her adventure to be a feast
of ripening cherries and peaches, Marseilles figs,
hot-house grapes, champagne shuddering in crystal.
Happiness, we believe, is on sumptuous display.
But unhappiness writes a different kind of play.
The gypsy gazes down into a clear blue crystal
and sees rotten cherries and withered figs.
Trust me: loneliness, too, can be a feast.

Ardor is delicious, but keep your own room.
One of my husbands said: is it impossible
for you to write a book that isn't about love,
adultery, semi-incestuous relations, separation?
(Of course, this was before our own separation.)
He never understood the natural law of love,
the arc from the possible to the impossible . . .
I have extolled the tragedy of the bedroom.

We need exact descriptions of the first passion,
so pay attention to whatever happens to you.
Observe everything: love is greedy and forgetful.
By all means fling yourself wildly into life
(though sometimes you will be flung back by life)
but don't let experience make you forgetful
and be surprised by everything that happens to you.
We are creative creatures fuelled by passion.

One final thought about the nature of love.
Freedom should be the first condition of love
and work is liberating (*a novel about love
cannot be written while you are making love*).
Never underestimate the mysteries of love,
the eminent dignity of not talking about love.
Passionate attention is prayer, prayer is love.
Savor the world. Consume the feast with love.

A Note About the Author

Edward Hirsch was born in Chicago, in 1950, and educated at Grinnell College and the University of Pennsylvania. His first book of poems, *For the Sleepwalkers* (1981), received the Lavan Younger Poets Award from the Academy of American Poets and the Delmore Schwartz Memorial Award from New York University. His second book of poems, *Wild Gratitude* (1986), received the National Book Critics Circle Award. His third, *The Night Parade* (1989), and his fourth, *Earthly Measures* (1994), were both listed as notable books of the year by *The New York Times*. He writes frequently for leading magazines and periodicals—among them *American Poetry Review, DoubleTake,* where he is editorial advisor in poetry, and *The Paris Review*—and he has received a National Endowment for the Arts Fellowship, an Ingram Merrill Award, a Guggenheim Fellowship, and the Rome Prize from the American Academy and Institute of Arts and Letters. He teaches at the University of Houston.

A Note on the Type

This book was set in a computer version of Granjon, a type named in compliment to Robert Granjon, type cutter and printer in Antwerp, Lyons, Rome, Paris. Granjon, the boldest and most original designer of his time, was one of the first to practice the trade of type founder apart from that of printer.

Linotype Granjon, of which this is a copy, was designed by George W. Jones, who based his drawings on a face used by Claude Garamond (1510–1561) in his beautiful French books. Granjon more closely resembles Garamond's own type than do any of the various modern faces that bear his name.

Composition by NK Graphics, Keene, New Hampshire
Printed and bound by Haddon Craftsmen,
  Bloomsburg, Pennsylvania
Designed by Harry Ford